TO JOHN

Merry Christmas

Stutto!

Statto's Ultimate Football Trivia Book

Also by Statto

Statto's Euro 96 Guide

Statto's Ultimate Football Trivia Book

Statto

HEADLINE

First published in 1996
by HEADLINE BOOK PUBLISHING

10 9 8 7 6 5 4 3 2

British Library Cataloguing in Publication Data

Loughran, Angus
    Statto's ultimate football trivia book
    1.Soccer – Miscellanea
    I.Title II.Ultimate football trivia book
    796.3'34

ISBN 0 7472 1845 5

Designed by John Hawkins
Printed and bound in Great Britain by
Mackays of Chatham PLC, Chatham, Kent

HEADLINE BOOK PUBLISHING
A division of Hodder Headline PLC
338 Euston Road
London NW1 3BH

Contents

Acknowledgements

S pecial thanks in compiling this project go to some great friends: Chris Rhys, whose help has been invaluable, and I thank him greatly. To soccer trivialist Alan Pedler from football hotbed Maeshafn in North Wales many thanks for some outstanding contributions. Thanks also to *Fantasy Football League* producer Andy Jacobs, who helped me compile the titles of each section and who has given me valuable support and encouragement since getting me involved in the programme; both professionally and personally I owe him much. Thanks also to Ray Spiller from the Association of Football Statisticians, Andy Porter whose knowledge of Tottenham is unrivalled, Oliver Lombard, and to new recruit Joseph Killingley. I hope the book gives you all the enjoyment that it has given me and my friends in its compilation.

Introduction

B eing an avid football fan ever since I can remember, and a collector of bizarre stories and trivia, I got my dream job when I was able to follow football around the world on a professional basis, reporting and commentating for Eurosport, ESPN and various publications. Then came my biggest break of all – as Statto hit the TV screens, working with Frank Skinner and David Baddiel on *Fantasy Football League*.

Things had come a long way from the day when I was taken to my first match, Manchester United v Burnley at Old Trafford in 1974, which I saw from the luxury of the executive suite. I knew I must like the game when my next match was watching non-League Altrincham, and was just as thrilled even if there wasn't the same atmosphere. In football I had discovered my passion in life, and Altrincham became my favourite non-League club.

Indeed, Altrincham were to set some sort of modern-day record when, in four consecutive seasons between 1979 and 1982, they reached the third round of the FA Cup. Their visit to Anfield in 1981, when they lost 4-1 but played with credit, still stands out in my memory.

As well as such highlights, Altrincham have also provided me with my most embarrassing football moment. I arrived on the supporters' coach at Droylsden for an FA Cup match and stood behind the goal in the pouring rain to cheer on my side in the hope they would once again reach the third round. I was naturally disappointed when the team in red went a goal behind during the first half, and as the players went in for the interval, I was hoping that Altrincham could stage a second-half fightback to gain at least a replay. I tuned in to *Sport on Two* to see how the other games were going and was astonished to hear it reported that Altrincham were winning 1-0. It suddenly dawned on me that I had been cheering the wrong team for 45 minutes!

Having been a fan for so long, you can imagine the thrill when I was recently made associate director of Altrincham, and I hope they can achieve their ambition and gain League status soon.

While there may have been some dodgy journeys to watch Altrincham, none can compare with the trip to South America where I was due to commentate on the second phase of the Copa America in Ecuador. I soon realised that my knowledge of some of the players was very limited. As all good Stattos should, I set out to remedy that by going to watch the sides in training, and attending the first two matches of the tournament: Ecuador v Venezuela in Quito and USA v Uruguay in Ambato.

The organisation was a shambles, so when I went on to the television gantry during lunchtime on the opening day I found a whole series of boxes placed where the television commentators from all over South America would be working. 'What's in them?' I asked the technical director.

'The TV monitors for the journalists,' he replied.

They didn't look like it to me, so I decided to open one of the boxes myself and investigate – they were microwave ovens! When the Brazilian commentator arrived an hour later, I wish I could have understood what he was saying, but judging by the amount of shouting and screaming he was not impressed.

There was also the occasion when Manchester United drew Dukla Prague in Europe. One player, when asked about the draw, commented with justifiable modesty: 'I have got to be honest; I don't know much about them, but it will be nice to go to a new city like Dukla.'

I decided to go to Prague by train – a journey which makes Shrewsbury to Norwich seem exciting. I arrived at the central station, where I decided to change some money, and then met up with some friends at a bar and ordered a round. So far so good. It was when I came to pay my bill that the problems arose – the currency I had been given went out of circulation over 50 years beforehand. I still owe the unknown British Telecom engineer from Stretford who bailed me out and saved me from a night in a Prague slammer.

Searching out the facts has helped in more than just tricky commentary situations, it has saved me when I was cornered in an

A glint in his eye, as Statto prepares to take on all-comers in a trivia battle.
(Graham Whitby/Sportsphoto)

Amsterdam pub. You wouldn't think that people would pick on a guy with glasses wearing pyjamas and a dressing gown, but the Dutch fans didn't like a Briton putting in an appearance in their home camp, especially as I could know nothing about their beloved club, Ajax, and its stars.

So I challenged them to a sporting duel, with 100 guilders (£40) as the prize: who could answer the most questions in a quickly arranged quiz on their club. The Dutch Statto, a lifelong Ajax fan, clogs shining brightly, got ready, half-chewed pencil in hand: this was a battle for the honour of Ajax, Amsterdam and Holland. By the end his pencil was snapped in half, and tears stained his clogs: he had been beaten! After that we settled down to a few drinks, and exchanged football stories. Proof, if proof were needed, that research is better than a black eye or a kick in the teeth.

The obsession with sport had started much earlier, and I remember how it first bore fruit during a general paper exam at Ampleforth. I had struggled through four of the five essays I was required to write when I was delighted to be able to write one on football: 'Tell the life story of Moses'. It started as follows:

'Remi Moses is a great player. He used to play for West Bromwich, where he was part of the Three Degrees with Laurie Cunningham and Brendon Batson, but he achieved his boyhood ambition by signing for Manchester United...'

You can imagine how surprised I was when a monk came up to me and told me I was writing about the wrong Moses! I apologised to him and explained I hadn't got all the information and the split times about Ed Moses, the 400m hurdler.

I still can't understand why the monk did not like my essay on Moses, seen here in action with Manchester United. (Colorsport)

I still get a huge buzz out of the game, and I hope that the money pouring into soccer at the moment will ensure that youngsters are not priced out of going to matches. Whatever the level of the match – and I have been to everything from the World Cup final to a non-League reserve game in recent months – there is so much to enjoy. I am already looking forward to the 1998 World Cup in France, which promises to be the best yet, not least because of the ever-increasing success of the African nations, culminating in Nigeria's Olympic triumph in Atlanta.

At whatever the level of involvement, once you're bitten by the bug of football it's almost impossible to ignore it. Jack Charlton may have feigned indifference, but as Johan Cruyff commented: 'Jack cracks me up. He makes out he is not really interested in football; he tells the whole world he is going fishing. But we know what he is thinking about when he is fishing: football.' While Aston Villa fans were mortified that anyone could make the heretical mistake that appeared on the cover of 'The History of Aston Villa' video: the team pictured there was in fact Burnley!

My footballing experiences have taken me to 212 grounds and over 3,000 matches in the last 20 years, and I am still looking for more new players to pick out, and more strange stories. Being with *Fantasy Football League* has obviously meant that a lot get sent in to us. That said, the questions I get asked most about the programme are: 'Do Frank and David really share a flat?' Yes they do, in Hampstead – and the set of the programme is modelled on it. Then others want to know if Uri Geller saw my drawing of England's Christmas tree formation before the programme. I can honestly say that to the best of my knowledge he did not. Perhaps the most difficult one of all to answer is 'What's the story with Jeff Astle?' Well, Jeff was one of Frank's heroes when he started watching West Brom, who began his singing career in the 1970 World Cup in Mexico, so that's how he got his chance with us.

What follows is a selection of the best trivia and quotes I have come across during that time. I hope they give you as much pleasure in reading them as they have given me in researching them.

Would You Believe It?

Some of Brazil's top clubs made interesting managerial changes in 1996 – the famous club Flamengo appointed a radio reporter with no training experience, while second division club Londrina appointed a star of TV soap operas. Londrina later declared that as they were bankrupt, the players' win bonuses would come in the form of cattle rather than money.

⚽

In the 1995-6 season, Barnsley fielded a Moses, an Archdeacon and a Bishop, despite which their prayers for a place in the Premiership were not answered.

⚽

Adrian Moses, part of the religious revival at Barnsley.
(Graham Whitby/ Sportsphoto)

Foxes shouldn't make themselves too much at home in football grounds, as this one found out to his cost at Wolves (appropriately enough!). (Colorsport)

Malaga, a former Spanish first division side, now rebuilding after a decade in the lower leagues, had a novel first prize in the club raffle – an hour with a prostitute.

✪

A family of foxes made their home in the main stand at Leyton Orient in summer 1995. They joined a group of wild cats.

✪

And another group of foxes took a liking to Chelsea's undersoil heating – apparently because worms flourished close to the piping.

✪

KR Reykjavik celebrated their 1995 Icelandic Cup win by pouring milk over their heads, as they are sponsored by a milk company. Champagne also costs £28 a bottle.

✪

There is a current trend among managers to stand up by the side of the dugout – but David Ashworth, Oldham's boss in the early 1900s used to run along the top of a small stand. The practice was stopped when he fell through the roof.

⚽

In Arsenal's first match at Highbury, players washed in bowls of water, and injured players had to be wheeled away in a milk cart.

⚽

During the 1995-6 season Blackpool installed a heated bench for their substitutes to sit on during the cold winter matches, with hot air blowing across the back of players' legs. The visitors get a hard wooden bench.

⚽

In the 1995-6 Spanish Primera Liga season, Valladolid won at Oviedo by 8-3. Six penalties were awarded and all were successful. Alen

The washing facilities at QPR in the 1970s showed little improvement on Highbury in 1913. (Mirror Syndication International)

Peternac, the Valladolid striker scored five goals including four penalties, while fellow striker Quevedo scored a hat trick. Three of the goals came in added time after 90 minutes' play.

Barcelona won 5-1 at Betis Seville in 1995-6. The match was held up because a rabbit dressed in a Betis green and white shirt took a great deal of cornering.

Dutch football fanatic Han van Eijden has a turnstile from Preston's ground in his garden at Almere.

Because of a colours clash, Blackburn Rovers played the 1890 Cup final against Sheffield Wednesday in evening dress shirts that they had brought for the reception on their trip to London.

Birmingham were offered bribes, of a sort, back in the 1870s. Their Muntz Street pitch was in such poor condition that opposing teams offered money to take the games elsewhere.

The Portuguese first division clubs Desportivo Chaves and Tirsense lost 4-1 and 5-1 over the same weekend in November 1995 and both teams complained of tiredness. It transpired that both teams had partaken of pre-match meals in the same restaurant, and the restaurateur is still protesting his innocence.

❂

Birmingham City used 57 players in first team games in 1995-6. They used a record 46 in League matches, hotly pursued by Torquay United who also broke the old record in fielding 43 players.

❂

Partick Thistle's 1995-6 game with Hibernian was postponed because of bad weather. The club had failed to switch on their undersoil heating.

❂

Albanian international players were banned by their own FA from swapping shirts in a Euro 84 qualifying match because they could not afford replacements.

❂

After the Falklands War, Stockport County considered changing their shirts from blue and white stripes because it was the colour of the Argentinian national team.

❂

Derek Ufton, the Charlton centre half, was taken to hospital after just 10 minutes of the game against Huddersfield in December 1957. When team-mate Stuart Leary visited him later in hospital, he was able to tell of a game in which the 10 men were 5-1 down; went 6-5 up; were pegged back to 6-6 and won in injury time with the 11th goal of the second half. Johnny Summers had scored four in a row for Charlton.

❂

Catholic priests at Celtic now have to pay to see tackles like this.
(James McCauley/Sportsphoto)

Catholic priests who support Glasgow Celtic in 1996-7 have been asked to pay to watch their team for the first time in 110 years. The club has replaced its free ticket policy for priests with a charity scheme for fans. The priests welcomed the move saying that they did not want any privileges at Parkhead.

❇

Portsmouth were the first club to run a creche.

❇

There are reports in the Stockport County fanzine that Manchester City have asked OJ Simpson's lawyers in. To sort out the defence...

❇

FIFA's Christmas card for 1995 had a team depicted on it. Nothing unusual except that there were 12 players in the team.

✪

In the 1960s the only bar to a club joining the League was that its ground should not be used for greyhound racing.

✪

The first computerised fixture list was produced by an ICL KDF9 computer in two minutes in 1968 – a total of 2028 matches.

✪

In the 1970s Scunthorpe obtained a minibus for transport by advertising for one million cigarette coupons from their fans.

✪

ITV once banned girls from entering their Penalty Prize competition as 'keepers are already under pressure, and wouldn't be keen having a girl hitting penalties past them. Also there is the problem of finding the girls a changing room at Wembley,' explained Mike Archer, editor of *On the Ball*.

✪

Preston will not play at home on Easter Monday because it would clash with the local Avenham Park egg-rolling tradition.

✪

Ghana's first division once comprised the following clubs: Hearts of Oak, Great Olympics, Kotoko, Hasaacas, Venomous Vipers, Mysterious Dwarfs, Cornerstones and Eleven Wise.

✪

'Wanderers Avenue' in Wolverhampton was named in recognition of the Wolves Cup-winning side of 1893. It contained 11 houses named after the team – Rose Villa, Brough Villa, Swift Villa, and so on.

✪

Blackpool's signature tune used to be 'Yes, we have no bananas'. It was abandoned for something more frivolous!

⚽

The term 'derby game' came from the Shrove Tuesday match in Derby between the parishes of All Saints and St Peter. Normally, about 250 a side played over fields, ditches, ponds and other natural obstacles.

⚽

Orient played two League matches at Wembley in 1930-31; their opponents were Brentford and Southend.

⚽

Arthur Chandler of Leicester scored in 16 successive matches in 1924-5.

⚽

Motherwell's Wales played for Scotland against Wales, while Mike England played for Wales against England.

Football's Happy Families

William 'Fatty' Foulke, the 6ft 3in tall, 22-stone legend who kept goal for Chelsea, among other clubs, often employed members of his family to retrieve the ball from behind the goal. He is believed to be the heaviest League player of all time. He wore size 12 boots and a 24in collar. He also played cricket for Derbyshire.

✪

From 1921 to 1961, the Yugoslav club Radnicki Pirot always had a member of the Zivkovic family in their side. When the record was broken in 1961, it was against a team who fielded all 11 players called Zivkovic.

✪

Forwards always found William 'Fatty' Foulke a hard keeper to get round – and if they did they were usually exhausted. (Colorsport)

At one stage the Wallaces threatened to form the whole team at Southampton – but in the end they left that role to Matt Le Tissier.
(Michael Atkelsky)

When brothers Danny, Rod and Ray Wallace all played several games for Southampton in the 1989-90 season, it was the first time that three brothers had played together in the same League side for 68 years.

❁

Back in 1908 Mrs Harrison gave birth to triplets on the same afternoon as husband William was scoring a goal for Wolves in the Cup final against Sunderland.

❁

Bobby and Jack Charlton won World Cup winners' medals in 1966 and then had one of the Queen's racehorses named Charlton in their honour.

❁

Bradley Allen, the Charlton forward, comes from the most distinguished of all football families. His father Les was in Spurs' 1961 Double team, and his brother Clive played for England. His uncle

21

Dennis also played for Charlton, as well as Reading, while Bradley's cousins are Paul, of West Ham, Tottenham and Southampton, and Martin, of QPR and West Ham. Of the six Allens, four played for QPR and three played for Spurs during their careers.

⚽

Ashley Ward, the Norwich striker, named his baby daughter Darby in February 1996. A month later he joined Derby for £1.2 million.

⚽

Former German international Rudi Voller's wedding to Sabrina contained no champagne celebrations. Voller wished to protest against French nuclear testing in the Pacific.

⚽

Father Arnor Gudjohnsen (aged 35) and son Eidur (aged 17) have both played for Iceland in 1996, Eidur having twice come on as substitute for his father. Their ambition is to start an international together. By the time you read this...

⚽

Brothers Tom and Tony English created a record of a wrong sort on 26 April 1986 when they were both sent off against Crewe in a fourth division game for Colchester United.

⚽

Bob Latchford of Everton scored League goals against his goalkeeping brothers Peter (West Brom) and David (Birmingham).

⚽

Well, they could be...
Luton Town's first game at Kenilworth Road on 4 September 1905 was dominated by the Greens. The opponents Plymouth wore their traditional green, the referee was a Mr Green, the game was kicked off by a member of the Greene King brewing family and the Luton club secretary was – yes, you've guessed it!!

Slip Of The Tongue

'In the other Euro 96 match Romania and Bulgaria drew 1-0.'
Moira Stuart, BBC newsreader

⚽

'Frank Spencer, the little Chelsea forward.'
BBC Radio 5 Live's Ron Jones – confusing John Spencer with the hero of Some Mothers Do 'Ave 'Em

⚽

Bruce Grobbelaar tries to slip on his tongue. (Richard Sellers/Sportsphoto)

Bobby Robson. (Colorsport)

'Newport County 0 Wrexham 1 – a good result for the Welsh.'
Radio 5 Live

❂

'The game could go either way and very nearly did.'
Jimmy Hill

❂

'And now the formalities are over, we'll have the National Anthems.'
Brian Moore, ITV

❂

'Plenty of goals in the lower leagues today – Hereford 0 Darlington 0.'
Radio 5 Live summariser

❂

'There are still hundreds of questionmarks to be answered.'
Jimmy Armfield, Radio 5 Live

⚽

'Everton's goal at West Ham was scored by Sammy Vinways.'
ITV Teletext

⚽

'Anything between 1-0 and 2-0 will be a good result.'
Bobby Robson

⚽

And a slip of the pen:

Crystal Palace match programmes contained three Craig Hignett photos, and captioned two of them as his lookalike Nick Barmby.

⚽

'I don't want to talk about last weekend's 3-2 draw at Bournemouth.'
Swindon manager Steve McMahon's programme notes

On Trivial Grounds

Barnsley's ground was considered to have too great a slope in 1898, so they moved 3000 cubic feet of soil from one end of the pitch to the other. It still slopes to this day – according to the fans away from the goal Barnsley are attacking, whichever it is.

❂

In 1942 Birmingham City's ground at St Andrews was destroyed by fire – by a fireman. The ground was being used as a wartime fire station and one of the braziers was dampened not by water, but by petrol.

❂

When Charlton first moved to The Valley, they had to change above a fishmonger's shop...

❂

... and when they tried to move back to The Valley in the early 1990s, the club's supporters entered candidates in the Greenwich council elections, polling nearly 16,000 votes. They were given permission to return to The Valley in 1991.

❂

Dundee (Dens Park) and Dundee United (Tannadice) are the closest league grounds in Britain, just 50 yards apart.

❂

Grimsby now play at Cleethorpes, the neighbouring town, but previously when at Clee Park, their first home ground, they had to change in the seaside beach-huts.

❂

A cow on the pitch at Pittodrie. No wonder the word means 'place of manure'. (Empics)

Aberdeen's Pittodrie Stadium was Britain's first all-seater stadium in 1980. Pittodrie means 'place of manure' as befits an area originally used as a dung heap by the local police horses.

⚽

Liverpool's Spion Kop is named after the famous battle in the Boer War where 322 British soldiers lost their lives in South Africa.

⚽

When Manchester City moved from their Hyde Road ground to Maine Road, they sold both stands to Halifax Town at the Shay ground – at a cost of £1,000. They are still there today.

⚽

Cynthia Payne, 'Madam Cyn', was a guest speaker at Leeds United's Elland Road ground in September 1995. Her specialist subject was 'Entertaining at Home'.

⚽

QPR hold the record for having had the most home grounds – 12 at present.

⚽

'Keep your nose out!' Eric Cantona and Steve Hodge discuss shirt sales at the Leeds club shop. (Popperfoto)

Tony Yeboah replica shirts sell at twice the rate that Eric Cantona replicas did at Leeds United's club shop.

⚽

In the 1980s Leicester City trained at Filbert Street under a huge plastic bubble to protect the pitch from the bad weather.

⚽

Norwich City's car park was used as a gun platform in World War II and manned by the local Home Guard.

Stoke City have been at the Victoria Ground for 118 years, a League record. No wonder it's now time to go!

❁

When Southend United's Roots Hall ground was excavated during World War I, the diggers found Anglo-Saxon remains and Viking coins.

❁

In 1919, Hartlepool built a temporary main stand to replace the one that had been flattened by a Zeppelin raid on 27 November 1916. It lasted until 1968.

❁

The roof of Chester's main stand at Sealand Road was sold to Port Vale.

❁

Wrexham's Racecourse is the only League ground to have its capacity determined by the number of toilets available.

❁

Arbroath's Gayfield is the League ground in Britain that is closest to the sea.

❁

The first heated stand was installed at Turf Moor, Burnley.

❁

Bristol City's Ashton Gate houses two indoor bowling greens under the Dolman Stand.

❁

When Stoke City bought the Victoria Ground from religious authorities, they agreed not to play there on the day of a religious festival.

❁

There were donkeys on the pitch at Villa Park long before Arsenal ever came to play there. (Colorsport)

At one of Aston Villa's early venues, Perry Barr, the players changed in a blacksmith's hut and there was a cluster of trees down one touchline.

Book The Referees

A referee, according to the FIFA fitness guidelines, will need to be able to run about eight miles during a game, and a linesman just over half that distance.

✪

Referee Ivan Robinson was responsible for the only goal of the Barrow v Plymouth Argyle match in November 1968. He accidentally deflected a shot from George McLean past Pat Dunne in the Plymouth goal and, by the laws of the game, the goal stood. He hurried off the field at the end to avoid congratulations from the Barrow players, and rather less warm applause from Plymouth.

✪

Referees need careful handling, as Ian Durrant finds out.
(Tony Edenden/ Sportsphoto)

Clive Thomas shows no mercy. (Colorsport)

Referee Clive Thomas incensed Brazilians when he disallowed a goal-bound shot by Zico in the 1978 World Cup against Sweden. The match was drawn 1-1...

⚽

...similarly in 1951, referee Bill Ling disallowed a West German equaliser against Ireland in Dublin, leaving the Irish winners by 3-2.

⚽

The referee for the 1878 Cup final was Mr Segar R Bastard.

⚽

Referees were paid at Cup finals from 1966 after they had been offered the choice in previous Cup finals of a medal or a fee and always chose the former. After 1966 referees were given both a medal and a fee.

⚽

In 1956 five long-term prisoners at Parkhurst Prison gained referees' certificates.

❂

Dutch referee Mr van Revens, who controlled the second leg of the Rangers v Sporting Lisbon European Cup-Winners' Cup tie in 1971-2, was suspended after the game had finished level on aggregate. He awarded a penalty shoot-out, which Rangers lost. But the club were reinstated as they should have been awarded the original game on away goals, having won 3-2 at home and lost 4-3 away. Rangers went on to win the Cup.

❂

Something similar happened on the opening day of 1984-5, when Sunderland hosted Derby County. The referee, Mr Kirkham, was late in arriving and a reserve referee took charge. When Mr Kirkham arrived (with Sunderland 3-0 up), he stopped the original game and started all over again. Luckily for him, Sunderland won 8-0 under his control and had in fact scored 11 times during a game of three halves.

❂

In September 1970 Alan Hudson 'scored' against Ipswich to help Chelsea to a 2-1 win. However, TV replays confirmed referee Roy Capey's worst nightmare – the ball had only struck the side netting. But the result had to stand.

❂

Hereford referee Jim Finney was forced to abandon the international between Scotland and Austria in May 1963 at Hampden Park because violent conduct from the visitors had led to three sendings-off. Mr Finney blew for the end of the game after 79 minutes saying that it was meant to be a friendly international.

❂

Referee Barry Knight had to leave the field when his jockstrap broke in the Beazer Homes League match at Ashford Town. When a

While naked referees are occasionally seen in the corridor, it is not normal practice for them to come onto the pitch with no clothes on. (Empics)

competition was run in the match programme the following week as to why the referee went off the field, it was won by the two tea ladies, who explained that they had seen a naked referee in the corridor.

⚽

England manager Graham Taylor uttered the now immortal phrase 'Do I not like that – you've cost me my job' as referee Assenmacher allowed Ronald Koeman to remain on the field in the Holland v England World Cup qualifier on 13 October 1993 following a deliberate foul on David Platt. Seconds later Koeman scored the first goal from a free kick.

⚽

Kim George, a Maths teacher from Bognor Regis, was the first woman to take charge of an FA Cup tie. She refereed the preliminary round game between Shoreham and Eastbourne on 3 September 1988.

✪

John Nielsen, of Scottish junior club Easthouses, was banned until the end of the 1996-7 season after being sent off against Civil Service Strollers and taking revenge on referee Kenny Low by cutting Mr Low's socks in half.

✪

Referee Kelvin Morton, an accountant from Bury St Edmunds, set a new British record when he awarded five penalties in the second division game between Crystal Palace and Brighton in March 1989. Palace had three first-half penalties inside five minutes, with Mark Bright scoring from the first and missing the second, and Ian Wright hitting the post with the third. After 50 minutes Brighton were awarded a penalty which Alan Curbishley converted but Palace's fourth penalty was then wasted by John Pemberton. Palace won 2-1, with all penalties being awarded in a 27-minute spell.

✪

Referee Steve Tomlin stopped the August 1995 Combination game between Crystal Palace and West Ham after 30 and 75 minutes for cricket-style drinks intervals. This was at the agreement of the clubs' trainers to combat 32°C heat.

✪

Steve Bucknor, the current international cricket umpire from the West Indies who stood in the 1996 England v Pakistan Test at Lord's, was a former FIFA international football referee.

✪

Referee Brian Martin had an unusual task to perform in the January 1979 FA Cup tie between Charlton Athletic and Maidstone. He had no option but to send off the Charlton forwards Derek Hales and Mike Flanagan for fighting each other.

✪

How to get sent off without being involved with another player. In the Libertadores Cup tie in March 1996, Ata Valencia of Ecuador's Espoli was playing against Barcelona, another Ecuador team, when he was given his marching orders for punching the driver of the injured-players' trolley, who had knocked him over on the way to attend to another player.

✾

Surprisingly few players take up a career as a referee – but Steve Baines of Chesterfield took charge at Rochdale on the opening day of the 1995-6 season. Baines played 436 games in a 10-year career that started at Nottingham Forest and finished at Chesterfield. Poacher turned gamekeeper, perhaps...

✾

...and Mark Halsey, another new League referee, was once bid for by Bobby Robson, who wanted to pay Hertford Town £10,000 for his services. Robson, then manager of Ipswich, rated the goalkeeper highly.

✾

Two referees in a match at the same time? – the experiment was tried in an England amateur international trial match in January 1935 at Chester. Referees Dr Barton (Repton) and Eddie Wood (Sheffield) officiated in each half, but the players were so well behaved that little was learned. Messrs Barton and Wood then refereed a professional trial between England and The Rest at West Bromwich Albion with similar lack of aggression from the players. The idea was then dropped, largely because the referees felt that they hadn't been involved enough as in a normal game.

✾

The referee of Glencraig United's match in February 1975 did not take long to get into the action: he booked all 11 players, plus the two substitutes, before the game started. He had been offended by the way they had chanted on his arrival.

✾

...and nearly a referee:

The linesmen at the 1996 Auto Windscreens final at Wembley were **Mr Kevin Pike and Mr Brian Fish.**

⚽

TV pundit Jimmy Hill, a qualified official, took over the line during the Arsenal v Liverpool match on 16 September 1972 after linesman Dennis Drewitt was injured.

Jimmy Hill takes over as linesman. Amazingly, some players argued with his decisions - how did they get a word in? (Mirror Syndication International)

FA Cup Runneth Over

Mrs Cadman, wife of a Tottenham director, began in 1901 a tradition that is continued today, that of tying the winners' ribbons to the FA Cup.

✪

Of the 11 players who took part in Tottenham's 1901 FA Cup success, Tom Morris was born closest to Tottenham, at Grantham, which is 100 miles away.

✪

The first player to score in every round of the FA Cup was Sandy Brown of Tottenham in 1901. His tally of 15 goals in the competition that season is a record that still stands.

✪

The first own goal in a Cup final was credited to Lord Kinnaird (Wanderers) in 1877. He was not given a ticking-off by team-mates as he employed most of them.

✪

The youngest player to play in the FA Cup is Andy Awford, for Worcester City against Boreham Wood, at the age of 15 years 88 days. Awford went on to play for England U21 and Portsmouth.

✪

Arthur Turner played in the 1946 FA Cup final for Charlton – though he was not the Turner who scored in both goals in that final. That honour fell to Bert Turner. But he has a record of his own: he made his debut in the Cup final, which was rare enough, but also had to wait four years to make his League debut. He moved to Colchester, who were not given League status until 1950.

✪

38

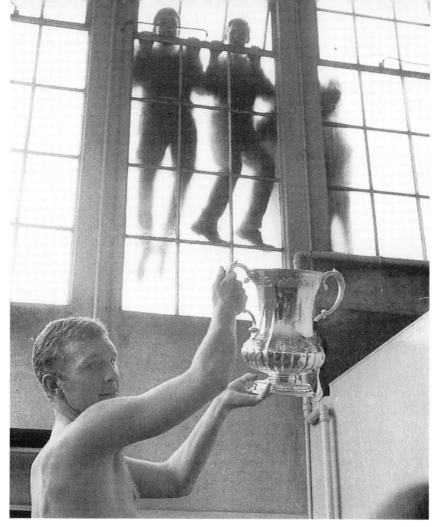

Bobby Moore caught in the act with a couple of accomplices trying to run off with the FA Cup after winning it in 1964. (Colorsport)

In 1911 the FA Cup was valued at £50.

❂

The original FA Cup was stolen from a shop in Birmingham on 11 September 1895 and never recovered.

❂

The record FA Cup score of 26-0 by Preston North End against Hyde on 15 October 1887 was not a 90-minute walkover. After 30 minutes the score was just 4-0.

⚽

The first club to win an FA Cup tie on a penalty shoot-out was Rotherham, who beat Scunthorpe 7-6 on penalties on 26 November 1991, after drawing 1-1 and 3-3.

⚽

Between 1945 and 1949, the Blackpool and England centre forward Stan Mortensen scored a goal in 12 successive FA Cup ties.

⚽

The 1996 FA Cup giant-killers Gravesend have a manager Chris Weller, whose home contains two iguanas, three parrots, a Thair water dragon and a monitor, which eats Pedigree Chum and will grow to 7 feet. Weller is an administrator at Rochester Prison.

⚽

Hereford United were banned from bringing their mascot to the 1996 FA Cup replay at Tottenham because of fears that it might be upset by crowd noise. The mascot was a one-ton bull called Free Town Kudos.

⚽

The longest FA Cup tie was the six games between Alvechurch and Oxford City in the fourth qualifying round during November 1975, which included visits to Alvechurch FC, Aston Villa FC, Oxford City FC, Birmingham City FC and twice to Oxford United FC grounds. ITV presenter Jim Rosenthal, who was at the time working for the *Oxford Mail*, reported on five of the six ties, and there was a commemorative tie issued to those who could prove that they had seen all six games.

⚽

Denis Law scored seven goals in a match and was on the losing side in a Cup tie. The Luton v Manchester City fourth round game was

*Denis Law celebrates another goal – but sometimes
even seven wasn't enough.* (Colorsport)

abandoned after 69 minutes with City leading 6-2. After Luton had taken a 2-0 lead, Law scored six in a row in 50 minutes. The replayed game on the following Wednesday also saw Luton take a 2-0 lead, and though Law scored again just before half time, the first-match avalanche did not materialise a second time and Luton ran out 3-1 winners.

⚽

In the three successive seasons from 1956-58 Cardiff City were drawn to play away at Leeds United. On all three occasions Cardiff came away from Elland Road with a 2-1 win.

⚽

In 1993, Arsenal became the first club to win both Cups in a season – the FA Cup and the League Cup. Sheffield Wednesday being the opposition on both occasions.

The Boy Done Good...
or strange

When Ian Rush scored his 200th League goal for Liverpool on 28 August 1993, he beat John Lukic of Leeds United. His first goal, scored 12 years earlier came against the Arsenal goalkeeper...John Lukic.

❁

While Ron Davies of Wales, Southampton and Norwich was also a cartoonist on the *Eastern Evening Mail* in Norwich.

❁

Paul Gascoigne's nickname at Rangers is Ticker – because he could explode at any moment.

❁

Gazza about to explode. (Allsport)

Peter Shilton and Ray Clemence, great rivals for the England No 1 shirt for over a decade. Shilts won 125-61. (Mirror Syndication International)

In May 1976, Peter Shilton asked not to be considered for England again, because, after 21 caps, he could not get a regular place in the national team owing to Ray Clemence's fine form. Shilton was to win 125 caps, a then world record.

❖

Terry Neill, Jack Charlton and Jimmy Hill were all members of the Boys' Brigade in their youth.

❖

Don Revie, 'Pop' Robson, Ronnie Simpson, Bobby Moncur and Peter Broadbent all won the Professional Footballers' Golf Championship during their careers.

❖

In the Nottingham Forest programme profiles, striker Paul McGregor was asked who he would most like to meet – the reply was: Steve Marriott of the Small Faces, Jim Morrison of The Doors and Elvis Presley. All three have sadly died.

❖

Terry Butcher comes off the pitch smiling after being daubed with the blood of a sheep in Turkey. No wonder Dalian Atkinson wanted to avoid this. (Popperfoto)

Dalian Atkinson's 1995 introduction to Turkish football was to be daubed with blood from a sheep slaughtered on the pitch. Atkinson tried to leave quietly, but was spotted and had to undergo the ritual.

⚽

Eric Cantona – part two

Romanian international midfielder Danut Lupu attacked a spectator in the stand during a 1995 league game after he had received abuse for missing an open goal. However, unlike Cantona, the victim was a Dynamo Bucharest supporter of Lupu's own team.

⚽

Bobby Moore was on the groundstaff of Essex County Cricket Club, while Geoff Hurst actually played one game for them against Lancashire. He scored 0 and 0 not out. Who knows? Had he had another chance he might have recorded a hat trick of a less honourable kind than the one at Wembley in 1966.

✺

Geoff Hurst's pre-match ritual meal was a plate of Welsh Rarebit.

✺

On the same day that he was named Footballer of the Year in 1960 by the FWA, Bill Slater of Wolves was dropped from the England side. He never played for them again.

✺

Ian Callaghan (Liverpool) went 11 years 59 days between successive England caps: his second came against France on 20 July 1966 during the World Cup, while his third was against Switzerland on 7 September 1977.

✺

Wives of Monaco and Paris St Germain players were summoned to meetings with a dietician after several players had over-indulged on French cuisine. Chief culprit was Bruno 'Fatty' Ngotty who had weighed a stone more since his move in summer 1995 from Lyon.

✺

The legendary Ferenc Puskas, star of the great Hungarian team of the 1950s, shows the effects of the Monaco and Paris St Germain diet. (Mirror Syndication International)

George Ley of Portsmouth won the competition for Most Attractive Footballer in 1968, gaining 40,132 votes. George Best was second with 40,129, and Eddie Gray of Leeds came third.

⚽

The next year, Gordon Livesey, Wrexham's goalkeeper who also played trumpet in the Wrexham Central Salvation Army Band, came second in the competition, behind Emlyn Hughes. George Best had slipped to third, but George Ley and Eddie Gray were clearly having a bad hair year.

⚽

England and Sheffield United winger Eddie Grainger also made a couple of records – for HMV. He went on to play a summer season at the seaside in 1957.

⚽

Bryn Jones of Arsenal always wore yellow socks when playing for Wales to make himself easier to find on the pitch.

⚽

Bobby Charlton won the £1000 jackpot on TV's *Double Your Money* answering questions on pop music.

⚽

Brazilian superstar and bad boy Edmundo was sent off in a 1996 game for Corinthians, who took a video of the incident to their FA in the hope of leniency. Unfortunately they took the wrong tape – and arrived at the hearing to show the adventures of Scooby Doo, a cartoon dog.

⚽

In 1995 Bournemouth signed Ryan Zico-Black, named after the Brazilian striker by his soccer-mad father. Bournemouth also gave a trial to Yazalse Santos, aged 20, who plays for Jersey Scottish because they don't have a Jersey Brazil.

⚽

Dixie Dean has scored most League goals in a season (60), which is a well-known fact, but the most in two successive seasons was by George Camsell (92), in three by J Cookson (124) and in four, five and six seasons by none other than Brian Clough (160, 194, and 223).

❄

Goalkeeper Vic Rouse of Crystal Palace was the first player from the fourth division to play in an international when he played for Wales against Ireland on 22 April 1959.

❄

Vivian Woodward was the highest scorer for Spurs in 1908-9 – he was also a director of the club. Improved goal bonuses were unanimously voted through the board that year!

What Are The Chances Of That Happening Again?

Marco Bochetti, of Italian non-league side Anzola, was booked in 1996 before he got onto the field. He was told by his trainer to warm up to come on as a substitute, and relieved himself behind the dugout before coming on to the pitch. He was booked for ungentlemanly conduct.

❄

On 22 January 1938, Barnsley's Frank Bokas scored a goal direct from a thrown-in via Manchester United keeper Tommy Breen's fingertips.

❄

Ron Atkinson and 'Deadly' Doug Ellis share a joke - what are the chances of that happening again? (Empics)

In January 1966, Port Vale played five teenagers in their forward line – Alex Donald (17), Paul Bannister (18), Roddy Georgeson (17), Mike Cullerton (17) and Paul Ogden (19).

⚽

Wales played internationals in 1953 with a forward line all of whom were born in Swansea – Terry Medwin, John Charles, Trevor Ford, Ivor Allchurch and Harold Griffiths.

⚽

Jack Froggatt and Stan Milburn, the Leicester City defenders, scored the only officially credited joint own goal against Chelsea in 1955.

⚽

Chelsea were elected to the Football League in 1905 without ever having played a competitive game.

⚽

In 1972-3 the divisional champions of the Football League all came from Lancashire – Liverpool, Burnley, Bolton and Southport.

⚽

In January 1959, Liverpool were beaten 2-1 in an FA Cup tie at Southern League club Worcester City. On a frozen surface, goals from Tommy Skuse and an own goal from Dick White were responsible for a result that surely can't happen again.

⚽

On 1 February 1971, Palermo midfielder Graziano Ladoni was fined £670 for failing to say goodbye in a courteous manner to his trainer. The Italian PFA objected to the fine.

⚽

Aston Villa defender Chris Nicholl scored all four goals in the 2-2 draw with Leicester City on 20 March 1976. Each time he put Leicester ahead with headed own goals before scoring for Villa with close-range shots. Nicholl had scored an own goal the week before.

⚽

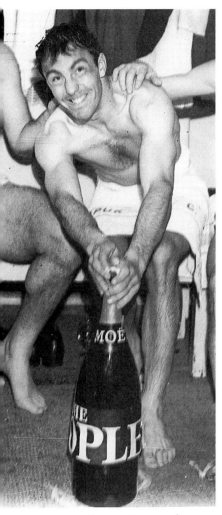

Jimmy Greaves always had plenty to celebrate, as he scored on debut every time. Here it is success in the 1962 FA Cup final that causes the corks to be popped. (Colorsport)

Jimmy Greaves scored on debut for West Ham United on 21 March 1970 to complete a record of scoring on debut for every League and international team for whom he had played.

George Hilsdon of Chelsea scored five goals on his League debut on 1 September 1906 against Glossop, the highest number of goals in a debut match.

Nine of Liverpool's 10 outfield players scored goals in an 11-0 European Cup-Winners' Cup tie against Stromgodset of Norway on 17 September 1974.

Substitute records are more difficult to chronicle but these records will take some beating:

– Goal after 10 seconds: Brendan O'Callaghan (Stoke) in 1979 on his League debut.

– Goal after 10 seconds of an international: Joe Craig for Scotland v Sweden, 27 April 1977.

– Sent off without touching the ball after coming on as sub: John Ritchie (Stoke) 1972, and Bobby Houston (Kilmarnock) 1979.

– All four substitutes scored in the Barnet v Torquay third division game on 28 December 1993 – Barnet won 5-4.

Vinny Jones ballet dancing to the Nutcracker Suite – *something that certainly won't happen again. He prefers morris dancing.*
(Mirror Syndication International)

The February 1996 open day at Real Madrid turned into chaos when 4,000 schoolgirls flooded across the pitch to mob their heroes.

⚽

Soren Lerby, the Bayern Munich and Danish international midfielder, played for his club team and for his international side on the same day – 13 November 1985.

⚽

In 1958 Lincoln City needed to win their last six games to have any chance of avoiding relegation to Division 3 North. They won all six games and managed to stave off relegation by a point.

❊

Stephane Moreau, the Caen defender, was booked for refusing to leave the field on a stretcher in a 1995-6 League Cup tie with Toulouse. A minute later he was sent off for a second bookable offence.

❊

Nine of the 11 first division games on 18 September 1948 were drawn.

❊

On Christmas Day 1936, Charlton Athletic and Sunderland drew 0-0. The remaining first division games were home wins.

❊

On 29 January 1937, there were 35 League and FA Cup games and not one produced an away win.

❊

On 3 October 1970, Ernie Hunt scored a fine goal for Coventry against Everton from an indirect free kick, set up by Willie Carr's 'donkey backheel', where he placed the ball between his ankles and flicked it up for Hunt to shoot. This trick has now been declared illegal.

❊

On 7 November 1931, Billy 'Ginger' Richardson, the West Brom forward, scored four goals in the first 10 minutes against West Ham in a 5-1 win. He scored his goals between the 5th and 10th minutes having missed two simple chances before opening his account.

❊

Christoph Daum, the Stuttgart trainer and Germany's answer to Brian Clough, accepted full responsibility for fielding four foreigners in a

European Cup tie against Leeds in the 1992-3 season. Leeds won the play-off game in Barcelona after being initially eliminated. Slobodan Dubajic was the fourth 'foreigner' used.

⚽

Luigi Coluccio was suspended for being sent off in a local league match in southern Italy in 1995. However, he had died nine days earlier in a mafia-related shooting. His club were told that the suspension would have to stand because of the league fair play awards at the end of the season.

⚽

On 12 November 1904, Everton were leading at Sheffield Wednesday by 5-0. Final score 5-5.

⚽

From 22 December 1962, the weather prevented any League football in England for nearly four months.

⚽

All snowed out at Birmingham – it gives the huskies something to do, as long as the Wolves stay away from the ground. (Empics)

Norwich City entered the 1904 FA Cup and made progress through four rounds to reach the third qualifying round. They then withdrew to play in the Amateur Cup.

The highest score in recent defensively dominated seasons has been the 20-0 win by Stirling Albion over Selkirk in the Scottish FA Cup in December 1984. David Thompson (7) and Willie Irvine (5) led the way as eight players scored. Selkirk keeper Richard 'Midge' Taylor might have had a chance to save only one shot on goal, the 13th, and there was a suspicion of offside about the 19th.

According to the original caption, Luton players and manager David Pleat 'gave up their bodies and their inhibitions to a team of beautiful masseuses at a health farm'. What are the chances of that happening again? (Mirror Syndication International)

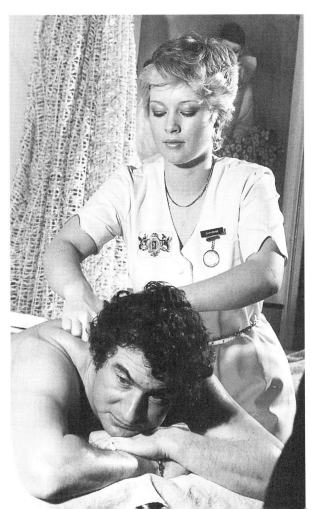

Many cup ties need a replay to decide a winner, but few in circumstances as bizarre as the Chester v Plymouth League Cup tie in September 1981. Then the goalpost snapped at its base when Grenville Millington, the Chester keeper, collided with the post in attempting to save Dave Kemp's shot after 78 minutes with the score 2-2. The teams met again the following week with the game finishing 1-1.

⚽

Goalpost damage forced a seven-minute delay at the Wolves v Bournemouth match in January 1957. Culprit Bournemouth's Reg Cutler later scored the winner in the replay as the third division side caused a major upset.

⚽

Even further goalpost damage occurred during the 1996 Spartan League game at Hanwell Town when four players ran in to meet a cross and dismantled the goal structures. The match was abandoned as an eye witness suggested that the players looked as though they were fish struggling to get out of a trawler's net.

⚽

The lowest number of games to be postponed because of the weather during a season was six in 1947-8; the highest number was 307 in 1962-3.

⚽

Hartlepool played the same defence and midfield in all 42 games in the promotion season of 1952-3: Wheeler, Staniforth, Kelly, McGarry, McEvey and Quested.

⚽

Dennis Allen of Charlton Athletic played for Malaysia against Mexico and Peru while on National Service.

⚽

When Reading played Rochdale in 1971 there were three Dennis Butlers playing, two for Reading.

☻

On 1 January 1966 both of Chester's full backs, Ray Jones and Bryn Jones, broke a leg in the game against Aldershot.

☻

Brentford goalkeeper Chic Brodie must have picked up the most unlucky career-ending injury of all time. The part-time taxi driver was forced to retire when a stray dog ran into his knee during a League game.

☻

Sheffield United's Dave Staniforth was looking forward to a quiet game on the subs' bench in a match against Chelsea, but when linesman Eric Read injured his leg, he was called upon to replace him.

Beat The Bar-room Bully

1 With which club did Michel Platini begin his first division career?

2 What did Steaua Bucharest, Auxerre and Atletico Madrid have in common in 1995-6?

3 Which ground was depicted in LS Lowry's 'Going to Match'?

4 Which former League club were nicknamed The Ironsides?

5 Who scored five goals for England in total, and they all came in one match?

6 How many times was the Scottish Cup tie in 1978 between Falkirk and Inverness Thistle postponed?

7 Which club did Cambridge United replace in the League?

8 Which was London's first professional club?

9 When England won the World Cup, who was voted Man of the Tournament?

10 Which famous player always wore No 14?

11 Which club were losing finalists in the first ever FA Cup final?

12 Which is the only club from the bottom division to reach a League Cup final?

Frank McLintock raises the FA Cup in 1971 – but what was unusual about how Arsenal got there? (Mirror Syndication International)

13 What was unusual about Arsenal's two Cup final appearances in 1971 and 1972?

14 Which three countries were granted four UEFA places for 1996-7?

15 Which two Spanish first division clubs were thrown out of the division for financial irregularities and then reinstated in 1995?

16 Who was top scorer in the 1995-6 Cup-Winners' Cup competition?

17 Who broke the record in 1995-6 for most goals in a season of European competition?

18 Which team had a 100 percent record in the 1995-6 Champions League group matches?

19 Who was top scorer for two successive seasons in the French second division?

20 In which year did Guy Roux take charge of 1996 French champions Auxerre?

21 True or false – Manchester United have never beaten Italian opposition in Europe?

22 Who was the last player before Alan Shearer to twice top the list of the Division1/Premiership goalscorers?

23 Who finished runners-up to promoted Middlesbrough in the 1994-5 Endsleigh League Division 1?

24 Four England players have won 100 international caps – but who is next in the order?

25 Which goalkeeper was unbeaten in League football for 1,103 minutes in 1979?

26 Who is second behind Kenny Dalglish as Scotland's most-capped player?

27 Who was the last Englishman to be Scottish Premier Division top scorer?

28 Which club ground is known as Paradise?

29 Which British team stages European matches at Farrar Road?

30 Four of his previous clubs all reached the 1996 French Cup semi-finals – who is he?

31 Who is the centre half who scored a hat trick against three different goalkeepers in the first division in 1985-6?

32 From whom did Jack Charlton take over as Ireland manager?

33 To which same club did five members of the West German team who won the 1954 World Cup belong?

34 Which was the last English club to win the Anglo-Italian Cup?

Jack Charlton celebrates in style after winning the Fairs Cup in 1971, carefully ignoring the can of shandy to his right – but who was his predecessor as Ireland manager? (Mirror Syndication International)

35 In which country are the quaintly named Red Boys one of the leading clubs?

36 Which player made his 100th international appearance during Euro 96?

37 In which years did England win the European U21 championship?

38 Who of England's Euro 96 squad once played for Besiktas in Turkey?

39 Which club won the first League of Wales title in 1993?

40 Which Euro 96 referee has a father who has trained a European Cup-winning side?

Record Breakers

They don't come much unluckier than Stockport County's Norman Wood back in 1913. He scored an own goal, he then conceded a penalty and then missed another penalty. Stockport lost 3-1 to Fulham.

❁

The only professional footballer to win the Victoria Cross was Donald Bell of Bradford Park Avenue. He won his VC for storming a machine gun in World War I.

❁

Preston North End have played on most League grounds.

❁

Birmingham City are the only club this century to have had a 100 percent home record – in 1902-3.

❁

The goal net was invented by Mr Brodie of Liverpool and first used in the match between the North and South in 1891.

❁

The first ever League Cup goal was scored by Maurice Cook of Fulham against Bristol Rovers on 26 September 1960.

❁

In 1898 Burnley and Stoke City played out a 0-0 draw to ensure that both remained in the first division. From that point the mini-league which operated for promotion and relegation was disbanded into a straightforward promotion/relegation format.

❁

Viv Anderson on his debut against Czechoslovakia at Wembley. England won 1-0 thanks to a Steve Coppell goal. (Colorsport)

The first black player to represent England in a full international was Viv Anderson on 29 November 1978.

⚽

The first goal in an FA Cup tie is credited to Jarvis Kenrick on 11 November 1871.

⚽

The League's first-ever own goal was scored by George Cox of Aston Villa against Wolves on 8 November 1888.

⚽

Who said that players were more sportsmanlike in olden times? In Bristol in 1904, the Bristol East keeper received a telegram to say that the match with Warmley was off. Bristol East arrived to play without a keeper, and the Football Association suspended three Warmley officials.

⚽

They don't score them like this anymore:

– Joe Payne (Luton) scored 10 goals against Bristol Rovers in a 12-0 win in April 1936. At one stage he scored nine goals in a 46-minute spell.

– Ted Drake (Arsenal) scored seven goals in eight attempts on goal in a 7-1 win at Villa Park against Aston Villa. His one miss was the seventh shot which hit the bar.

– Wilfred Minter scored all seven goals for St Albans in a fourth qualifying round FA Cup replay at Dulwich Hamlet in November 1922. Minter's side was 3-1 up, then 5-3 down, then 6-5 up and 6-6 at 90 minutes. The score reached 7-7 during extra time before Davis of Dulwich Hamlet scored with the last kick of the game.

⚽

Adams, challenged by Fashanu, tries to prevent Arsenal from conceding yet another goal from a corner. (Colorsport)

Barry Lines scored for Northampton Town in all four divisions.

❂

Mrs M E Montague was the first woman secretary of a League club when she was appointed by Crystal Palace in the late 1950s.

❂

The penalty shoot-out decider was first used in England in Watney Cup matches in 1971-2.

❂

Ardwick (later Manchester City) are believed to be the first club to issue a match programme.

❂

The first League goal scored direct from a corner was by Billy Smith of Huddersfield against Arsenal in 11 October 1924. Ever since then, Arsenal have signed up all tall centre halves to prevent any repetition!

What's In A Name?

Middle names:

England star Paul Ince's are Emerson Carlysle
Spurs and England legend Martin Chivers' is Harcourt
Southampton's Ted Bates was actually christened Edric Thornton

Paul Emerson Carlysle Ince grasses up Marco Grassi, who was picking on him for his unusual middle names. (Popperfoto)

A pineapple. (Mirror Syndication International)

Some fruity players:

George Berry of Wolves and Queens Park Rangers
Trevor Cherry of Huddersfield, Leeds United and England
Steve Grapes of Norwich, Bournemouth and Cardiff
Jason Lee of Charlton, Lincoln, Southend and Nottingham Forest
Arthur Lemon of Nottingham Forest
David Peach of Gillingham, Southampton and Swindon
Jeff Pears of York City

Very fishy characters:

David Bass of Reading
Ronnie Codd of Bolton Wanderers, Sheffield Wednesday and Barrow
Andy Flounders of Hull
Steve Guppy of Wycombe and Port Vale
Andrew Haddock of Chester, Crewe, Bradford PA and Rotherham
Harry Herring of Hartlepool
Joe Mullett of Norwich
Geoff Pike of West Ham United
Edward Rudd of Accrington Stanley
Len Salmon of Tranmere Rovers
Lee Smelt of Nottingham Forest
Tommy Spratt of Bradford PA, Torquay, Workington and Stockport

Some total animals on the pitch:

Len Badger of Sheffield United
Frank Bee of Sunderland and Blackburn
Alan Buck of Colchester
Steve Bull of Wolves
Micky Bullock of Orient
George Duck of Southend
Ruel Fox of Tottenham Hotspur
Steve Fox of Wrexham
Malcolm Gibbon of Port Vale
Tom Hare of Southampton
Harry Lamb of Tranmere
Jimmy Seal of York

Great birds:

Alan Eagles of Orient
William Heron of Gateshead
Albert Nightingale of Huddersfield and Leeds
Don Partridge of Rochdale

Darren Peacock tries to take flight. Will he dye his hair iridescent blue to complete the effect? (Colorsport)

Darren Peacock of Newport, Hereford, QPR and Newcastle United
Pete Phoenix of Oldham
Richard Rook of Middlesbrough
John Sparrow of Chelsea
Ron Starling of Aston Villa
Peter Swan of Sheffield Wednesday
Colin Swift of Barnsley
John Wren of Rotherham

Players to help you win at Scrabble:

Dariusz Dariuszdowczyk of Reading
Mark Dziadulewicz of Wimbledon
Rick Kwiatskowski of Peterborough
Steve Wojciechowicz of Blackpool
Dick Kryzwicki of West Bromwich

Oddbods:

Fred Blackadder of Carlisle
Tunji Banjo of Orient
Forbes Phillipson-Masters of Plymouth
William Mustard of Exeter
Arthur Potty of Northampton
William Tulip of Darlington

❇

Referee Leo Callaghan called his house 'Offside'.

❇

In 1934 and 1937 two World Cup qualifying matches involving Hungary v Bulgaria and Lithuania v Latvia were refereed by Herr Frankenstein of Austria.

❇

Bobby Moore named his Siamese cat Pelé.

❇

The Grimsby firm Consolidated Enterprises named their trawlers after 15 League clubs, plus Real Madrid, the first being *Blackburn Rovers*. *Notts County* sank in an Icelandic port, and *Aldershot* and *Everton* were involved in the Cod War.

Coming Home To Euro 96

Why did England wear those unlucky grey shirts, so hated by Manchester United, in Euro 96? The sponsors, Umbro, said that with Manchester United, Liverpool and Arsenal all wearing red shirts, there were too many replica red shirts about.

⚽

Accident count after Turkey's 2-2 draw with Sweden which qualified them for their first major finals since 1954 – two dead of heart attacks, three wounded by stray bullets, and 80 arrested for firing guns in the streets.

⚽

Dutch defender Johan de Kock is a civil engineer in Limburg, planning new by-passes, while Sebastian Jeanneret, the Swiss defender is... yes, you've guessed it... a clock repairer.

⚽

Not surprisingly, given his hobby, Sebastian Jeanneret (No 13) arrives just in time. (Colorsport)

England's matches were dominated by penalties – in the opening game Swiss striker Kubilay Turkyilmaz scored the equaliser from the spot, then in the next game David Seaman saved Gary McAllister's penalty against Scotland. In the final group game Alan Shearer opened the scoring against Holland from the spot, while the quarter-final against Spain and semi-final against Germany were decided by penalty shoot-outs.

⚽

Euro 96 gained an unenviable record as the most card-ridden tournament in history. There were 157 yellow cards shown and seven players were sent off. The record was 10 bookings in the Germany v Czech Republic group match, which was refereed by England's David Elleray.

⚽

The biggest crowd at Euro 96 was the 76,684 fans who attended the England v Scotland match, while the biggest attendance outside Wembley was 53,740 at Old Trafford for the Group C game between Italy and Germany.

⚽

The 31 Euro 96 matches were watched by 1,268,201 spectators, an average of 40,916 per game.

⚽

Aron Winter, former team mate of Paul Gascoigne at Lazio, was surprised and delighted when Gazza's stretch limousine drew up outside the Dutch hotel to take Winter and half a dozen of his team-mates to London's Planet Hollywood for lunch.

⚽

John Gorman, who was appointed No 2 to Glenn Hoddle in the England training set-up, was refused admission to St James' Park media centre. No one recognised him.

⚽

Holland won the UEFA Fairplay Best Fans award, due largely to their splendid brass bands – Half a Pint and the Orange Hooters. Harry Verdonck, leader of the Hooters, explained their success: 'It's simple. If the fans sing, then they don't fight.'

The Bulgarian squad, despite a £30,000 incentive from the local council at Scarborough in the hope that it might encourage their fans to visit the town, left their hotel ahead of schedule because of boredom and the long journey to matches. They booked into another hotel at Stockton. The Bulgars couldn't hack Stockton either, and, after two more nights, decamped to the Romanian squad's HQ at Redworth Hall, County Durham.

Romania's early exit proved a blessing in disguise for devoted fan Constantin Cuica, who walked from Bucharest to Newcastle to support his team. He immediately had all his belongings stolen from a campsite in Newcastle, and when locals came to the site with peace

Gheorghe Hagi asks the linesman if he has seen Constantin Cuica's belongings. (Colorsport)

offerings, they were unable to find him. However, one of Cuica's friends soon explained: 'He's left already. He's on his way to Atlanta to walk to the Olympics.'

☸

Czech Republic midfielder Vladimir Smicer had no idea that his team would reach the final of Euro 96, or that he might be part of the final. He arranged his wedding in Prague, to the daughter of former international Ladislav Vizek, for the Friday before the final. Smicer was allowed home to marry after the semi-final win over France, and postponed his honeymoon until after the Wembley final.

☸

The Italian squad were unhappy with their Euro 96 training headquarters at Crewe and Alsager College and got together to pay half the £20,000 needed to upgrade facilities. Much of the money went towards new showers, mirrors and hairdryers so that the squad could 'look the business' as well.

☸

With the Russian general election taking place during Euro 96, the squad were allowed to fax their vote to the main polling station.

☸

Denmark played all three of their group games at Hillsborough. As a mark of respect to the 95 people killed in the 1989 Hillsborough disaster, the Danes wanted to play in the blue and white strip of host club Sheffield Wednesday. But the plan hit red tape with UEFA regulations concerning strip and sponsorship.

☸

Bookmakers William Hill thought they had a record bet on their hands when a punter wanted to put '40 million' on Italy to beat Germany. Further questioning, though, revealed the amount to be in lira, not pounds sterling. Even so, it was still a bet of about £16,000.

☸

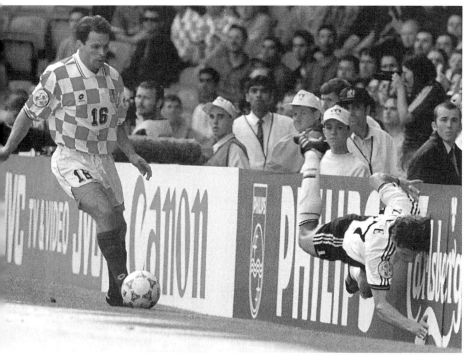

Christian Ziege of Germany, probably the best team in the world, is desperate for a Carlsberg, probably the best lager in the world. (Popperfoto)

Goran Vlaovic, the Croatian striker, who played in Italy for Padova, had life-saving brain surgery some six months before Euro 96. His guest of honour at the finals was the Belgian surgeon who saved his life.

❊

Euro 96 was the biggest sporting betting bonanza in British history. Over £80 million was staked on the event, with the England v Scotland match alone attracting bets of £8 million.

❊

The sports editor of the Romanian TV station at Euro 96 was so impressed with Darlington that he wanted to buy a house there.

✪

Holland brought to Euro 96 the following items:

900 pairs of shorts	100 tracksuits
550 pairs of socks	100 pairs of bootlaces
550 shirts	140 jockstraps.

✪

The French brought 360 bottles of wine with them via Le Shuttle, courtesy of Bixente Lizarazu, the Bordeaux full back, who has a major share in a vineyard.

✪

In the Dutch press release for Euro 96, winger Gaston Taument was 'the father of a twin'.

✪

On the night England lost to Germany in Euro 96, the England rugby league team were winning their European Championship at Cardiff Arms Park.

✪

Scotland gained immediate revenge during Euro 96 for their group defeat by England by winning the match between English and Scottish MPs by 4-0. Like the real one, the England keeper Teresa Gorman had a good game.

✪

One of the Russian squad at Euro 96 was almost left behind at departure time. An unnamed player, after a final-night party, was found by a chambermaid fast asleep in his room some 20 minutes after the bus had left for the airport. The hotel manager phoned the team coach to tell them they had left one behind, and they hadn't even noticed.

✪

Oliver Bierhoff, Germany's two-goal hero in the final of Euro 96, trained as an opera singer before opting for football.

⚽

Inhabitants of the small village of Ysno Pole have voted to change its name to Stoichkovo in honour of Hristo Stoichkov, who was born in the village. They have sent their petition to the President of Bulgaria, Zhelyo Zhelev.

Hristo Stoichkov suddenly realises that if he keeps on going like this, they'll rename Sofia after him, too. (Colorsport)

Great Personalities

Eric Morecambe's directorship at Luton Town was the fulcrum of many jokes and sketches in the *Morecambe and Wise Shows* on BBC Television.

❂

John Major, just before he became Prime Minister, had to delay his family holiday in 1990 to enable his son James to have a trial with Aston Villa. James now works for Marks and Spencer. Mr Major and former government minister David Mellor are staunch Chelsea supporters.

❂

TV commentator Alan Parry is a director of Wycombe Wanderers, while Brian Moore was a director of Gillingham.

❂

Comedian Norman Wisdom was a director of Brighton and Hove Albion, Eric Sykes was a director of Oldham Athletic, and Bobby Ball was on the board at Rochdale.

❂

England cricket captain Colin Cowdrey was a director of Charlton Athletic.

❂

A charity fund-raising team of the late 1950s included Sean Connery as inside left, and Des O'Connor as right wing in the Show-Biz XI.

❂

A comedian and Tommy Trinder together at Fulham.
(Mirror Syndication International)

Older readers would remember internationally famous comedian Tommy Trinder as chairman and president of Fulham.

❇

Film star Peter Sellers was an honorary vice-president of Wood Green FC in the late 1950s at the time of the Goon Show.

❇

Charlie Williams, comedian and TV compere of the 1970s, played for Doncaster Rovers.

❇

Neil Paterson, who won an Oscar for his screenplay of the 1960 film *Room at the Top*, was captain of Dundee United in the 1936-7 season.

⚽

Former Conservative MP Jack Slater played full back for Bolton Wanderers before World War I.

⚽

FIFA international referee Denis Howell (later Lord Howell) was a Labour MP and Minister for Sport. He was also probably more famous as the Minister for Drought in the hot summer of 1976.

⚽

Well at least the name's the same:

Charlie Chaplin was a reserve keeper for Wolves between the wars.

Neville Chamberlain played League football for Port Vale and Stoke City and is international forward Mark Chamberlain's brother.

Neville Chamberlain calls for the ball: 'Pass in our time.'
(Hulton Deutsch Picture Collection Limited)

Ray Charles, the Montrose goalkeeper, makes you wonder why they ever tell jokes about Scottish goalies. (Redferns)

Anthony Eden played for Aston Villa and Walsall.

Winston Churchill played a couple of junior games for Chelsea in 1956.

Ray Charles was the keeper in Montrose's 1984-5 Scottish Division Two championship win.

⚽

Retired double Olympic gold medallist Daley Thompson spent 1995-6 on the books of Mansfield Town.

⚽

Michael Caine (Captain Colby) and Sylvester Stallone appeared in the 1980 football film *Escape to Victory*. More familiar names included Pelé, Bobby Moore, Ossie Ardiles and several Ipswich players, who gained their first caps for Germany in the film.

⚽

The actor Alan Rothwell (David Barlow in *Coronation Street*) used to work on Oldham Athletic club radio.

⚽

Bill Tidy used to provide cartoons for the Queens Park Rangers match programme.

⚽

The singer Tom Jones became president of Newport County in 1969.

Who Said That?

Lord Nelson, Lord Beaverbrook, Sir Winston Churchill, Sir Anthony Eden, Clement Attlee, Henry Cooper, Lady Diana. We have beaten them all... Maggie Thatcher, your boys took a hell of a beating.'
Norwegian TV commentator Borge Lillelien, on his country's 2-1 win against England on 9 September 1981

❁

'F...... off, Norway.'
Paul Gascoigne to TV reporter on 12 October 1993 having been asked if he had a message for that country on their qualification for the 1994 World Cup finals

❁

'I hear Vinny Jones has learned the Welsh national anthem. He can learn the French one too if we get to the 1998 World Cup finals.'
Bobby Gould, new Wales manager

❁

Vinny Jones, his Welsh temperament showing through, goes in hard on five-year-old Robert Kelly. (Mirror Syndication International)

'Dalglish will never make it in English football – he's too weak and hasn't got the skill or temperament for our game.'
Terry Neill, Arsenal manager in 1977, after being offered Dalglish for a mere £100,000 by Celtic manager Jock Stein

⚽

'Mr Whelan is a God. Wigan will be in Division One in two years.'
Roberto Martinez, one of three Spaniards taken in by owner Dave Whelan

⚽

'I'm going to tape *Neighbours* over this.'
Harry Redknapp after West Ham's draw with Southampton, 1995

⚽

'I know we were 4-1 favourites for relegation, I had a tenner on it myself.'
Harry Redknapp, West Ham manager, on his club's prospects for the 1995-6 season

⚽

'We're both from Dagenham so we get on fine.'
Paul Ince, on his alleged disagreement with England manager Terry Venables

⚽

'I play with passion and fire. I have to accept that sometimes this fire does harm. I cannot be what I am without these sides to my character.'
Eric Cantona, on his comeback after an eight-month ban

⚽

'We always know exactly what to expect and it is easy to prepare against English teams.'
Nils Arne Eggen, Rosenborg coach, after his side's 2-1 Champions League win against Blackburn

⚽

'What's this?' asks Wolves manager Graham Taylor. 'It's a ball, boss.'
Soon after, Taylor was gone. (Tony Edenden/Sportsphoto)

'Iain's a bright lad – he's got a degree in engineering, and if any of the lads has a problem with their car, I'm sure he'll give expert advice.'
West Ham captain Steve Potts' welcome to new signing Iain Dowie

❁

'You cannot be serious.'
Barbara Clough, after hearing rumours that Brian Clough was interested in the vacant Wolves post after Graham Taylor was sacked

❁

Ruud Gullit checks to see why it is he's squealing so much. (Empics)

'They don't squeal as much as Ruud Gullit.'
Vinny Jones, on owning pot-bellied pigs

⚽

'Even then he was off his head – he would keep sweets in his socks and then give them to the teachers to eat.'
Steve Stone on schooldays with fellow international Paul Gascoigne

⚽

'The sort of money being bandied about for Trevor wouldn't buy his boots.'
QPR manager Ray Wilkins on the bids for Trevor Sinclair

⚽

'I don't understand it – we did everything right in training.'
Torquay manager Don O'Riordan, sacked after an 8-1 home defeat by Scunthorpe in 1995

⚽

'Thief stopped play.'
Headline in local paper at Twickenham when teams from St Mary's and St George's medical schools spotted a thief with their valuables bag, and gave chase. The British Universities Championship match was abandoned through darkness when players returned from the chase

⚽

'If you are the President of Real Madrid, Barcelona or AC Milan, then I'll get back to you .'
Wimbledon manager Joe Kinnear's answerphone message at home

⚽

'It may sound daft, but until we let in three goals just before half time, I thought we were the better side.'
Roly Howard, after Marine were knocked out of the 1995-6 FA Cup at Shrewsbury. Final score 11-2

⚽

'It's his own style that he has developed over the years.'
BBC Radio's Head of Sport Bob Shennan after commentator Alan Green gave out the result of his son's cub match over the air

⚽

'I still like to keep in touch.'
Newcastle United defender Darren Peacock, who sponsors kit for his first club, Newport County – now Newport AFC

⚽

Graeme Le Saux and David Batty discuss tactics during Blackburn's game against Spartak Moscow. (Empics)

'Before the game I said the usual stuff – play for 90 minutes, and it's 11 against 11, and to go out and fight. I didn't say fight with each other.'
Ray Harford, Blackburn manager on the Graeme Le Saux v David Batty set-to in the Champions League game with Spartak Moscow

⚽

'If it moves you kick it; if it doesn't move you kick it until it does.'
Phil Woosnam describing the basics of football to Americans

Boring But True

Queen of the South's current shirt logo includes the large letters OU. The Open University are the sponsors – but no money changed hands apparently – just publicity for the OU in the local community.

❖

Leeds United were so impressed by the great Real Madrid European Cup-winning side of the 1950s that manager Don Revie changed the club's colours to all white as a mark of respect for the European Cup holders.

❖

Colin Peake, the man who invented the rubber-handled linesman's flags, was once a policeman who worked on the notorious Frederick and Rosemary West 'House of Horrors' murder case.

❖

When Fulham left the Southern League (the regional forerunner of today's second and third divisions), they were replaced by a Yorkshire club, Bradford Park Avenue.

❖

The first penalty in the Football League was awarded to Wolves against Accrington on 14 September 1891. John Heath scored from the spot.

❖

The Brazilian FA committed an enormous *faux pas* in selection for the 1995 international with Argentina. Coach Mario Zagalo selected Leandro of Botafogo but the Brazilian FA contacted Leandro of Inter

*A snow of confusion surrounded Ian Walker's selection
for the England squad in April 1996. (Empics)*

Porto Alegre instead. It was only when he was being interviewed on
TV that the error was noticed...

❄

The FA committed the same *faux pas* in April 1996 when BBC Radio
Sheffield correctly at the time interviewed Des Walker on his return
to the England squad. A hurried fax revealed the player should have
been Tottenham's Ian Walker.

❄

In 1995-6 Ipswich fans could buy a match ticket from any one of the
200 Greene King public houses.

❄

A Betis Seville fan takes his father's ashes to every home game as requested in his will. He still has a seat in the stand and the Betis club put the ashes in a milk carton. The son shakes his father's ashes as a ritual every time Betis score a goal...

⚽

...and Ajax members' ashes can be scattered on their old pitch for £100 after the Westgaarde cemetery bought the old ground. Ajax moved into their new stadium, the Amsterdam Arena, in August 1996.

⚽

Chelsea were the first club to produce a 16-page match programme in December 1949. They also hold the record for most programme sales for a League match, 62,586 against Manchester United.

⚽

In 1899 Tottenham changed their strip to the current white shirts and blue shorts as a mark of respect to Preston North End, the most successful team of that era.

⚽

The first club shop to be open six days a week was Birmingham City's Beau Boutique.

⚽

The first World Cup tie on a synthetic surface was not in the 1994 finals in the USA but a qualifier between Canada and USA on 24 September 1976 at Vancouver. The return match was also unusual, the Seattle Kingdrome hosting the first World Cup tie indoors on 20 October 1976.

⚽

The international record for a penalty shoot-out is the 1975 Asia Cup semi-final between Hong Kong and North Korea. The teams were level 3-3 after extra time and some players were on their second round of penalties when North Korea eventually won 11-10 on penalties. There were 28 penalties taken, seven of which were unsuccessful.

⚽

Mount Hodge, a major battleground of the Falklands War, once had the best football pitch on the island at its base.

⚽

A Wartime Cup tie between Stockport County and Doncaster Rovers was played to a finish, at least it should have been – but after 203 minutes, with the score 2-2, the referee called the game off because of bad light. Doncaster won a hastily arranged replay 4-0.

⚽

Tom Finney's face is painted onto the seats of the new Tom Finney stand at Preston's Deepdale.

⚽

The biggest transfer discrepancy? Andy Walker's move from Bolton to Celtic in 1994. Bolton wanted £2.2 million, Celtic bid £220,000. The tribunal fee – £550,000.

⚽

The record for keeping a football in the air is held by Sam Ik of South Korea – 18 hours 11 minutes and 4 seconds.

⚽

Arsenal's original name was Dial Square, named after one of the workshops in HM Government's Royal Arsenal arms factory at Woolwich, south-east London.

⚽

The reason Arsenal wear red shirts is that their original kit was donated by Nottingham Forest, who also gave them their first ball.

⚽

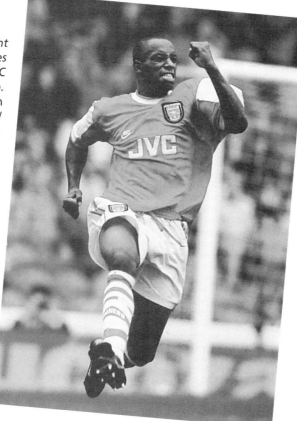

Ian Wright celebrates Arsenal's JVC sponsorship. (Shaun Botterill/ Allsport)

Arsenal are the only Premiership club to have retained their original shirt sponsors – JVC – since sponsorship began in the 1980s.

❖

Police are looking for an Arsenal-hating Chelsea fan – the reason being that while breaking into a London office, he had time to alter the office sweepstake ladder to put Chelsea top and Arsenal bottom.

❖

When Inter Milan finally sold former Golden Boot winner Darko Pancev to Fortuna Dusseldorf, they thought it was the end of his unhappy spell in Italy. But, with the lifting of FIFA sanctions on Pancev's former club Red Star Belgrade, the club asked Inter for the

Darko Pancev heads Inter Milan into financial trouble. (Colorsport)

£6 million that they had never received when he left them. It was the final blow.

❁

Dave Hutchings has probably seen more football grounds throughout the world than any other living person. His July 1996 schedule included a three-week holiday in Iceland so he could visit all 10 league grounds there.

❁

The fastest trip round the 93 different League grounds is 237 days in 1995 by Ken Ferris. When asked whether he thought his record would be beaten Ferris replied that he thought so, as he had taken a two-week holiday in the USA when setting his record.

❁

The smallest League player is believed to be Fred le May, who played for Thames, Watford and Orient, who measured just 5ft.

☸

Preston North End introduced professionalism into football when they began paying their Scottish players in 1885.

☸

Manchester City were relegated from the first division in 1938 despite being the top goalscorers in the League with 80, three more than champions Arsenal.

☸

Most boring game of all time? The Newcastle v Portsmouth match on 5 December 1931 must be a candidate. Not only was it a 0-0 draw, there wasn't even a single corner kick in the whole game.

☸

Plymouth Argyle were so named after being formed in a house in Argyle Terrace in 1886.

☸

Fred Davies used to be paid five shillings for every ball he retrieved from the River Severn behind Shrewsbury's Gay Meadow. His boat improved over the years from a coracle to a motor launch…

☸

…while Fulham employed maintenance man Peter Woolgarth to shoot pigeons with an air rifle at Craven Cottage.

☸

The then Second Division Cup melted down in the Cardiff City fire of 1968.

☸

A football was used as a crest on the coat of arms of Sir William Jordan of Chitterne in Wiltshire as early as 1622.

Bobby Charlton receives a kiss from his mother, which meant he had to take his cigarette out of his mouth. (Mirror Syndication International)

In his prime, Bobby Charlton smoked ten cigarettes a day 'but none until training was over at two o'clock' according to *Woman* magazine.

❖

The last non-League player to win an England cap was Edgar Kail of Dulwich Hamlet in 1924. He played against France, Belgium and Spain.

❖

In 1910 the Football League had to step in to prevent Fulham from taking over Arsenal.

❖

Only one game has ever been postponed because of high winds: Bolton Wanderers v Sheffield Wednesday on 22 December 1894.

Mastermind

1 Who first took over from Diego Maradona in the No 10 shirt for Napoli?

2 Who is the youngest player to be sent off in the World Cup finals?

3 Which English club won the Anglo-Italian Cup in 1979?

4 In which year did four Britons appear in the Italian Cup final?

5 Which British club play their home games at Seaview?

6 Which venue staged the World Club Cup immediately before Tokyo?

Maradona's daughter eyes up his No 10 shirt – but who actually took it over? (Colorsport)

7 Which name has been both South American and African Footballer of the Year?

8 Who was runner-up to the great Alfredo Di Stefano in the 1957 European Footballer of the Year award?

9 Which was the first club to win the European Cup final on penalties?

10 What was significant about the 1996 European U21 Championship semi-final between Italy and Portugal?

11 Which was the first Scottish team to float a share issue on the Stock Exchange?

12 Who scored a hat trick of penalties against Coventry in 1986?

13 In which year was the Queen last at the Cup final as Guest of Honour?

14 Which is the only year that 'Abide With Me' has not been sung at a Wembley Cup final?

15 Which club has been twice European Cup finalists in a four-year spell and is now defunct?

16 What claim to fame has Italian trainer Vittorio Pozzo?

17 Who scored the first golden goal in senior English soccer?

18 Which England managers have suffered just one defeat in their time with the national side?

19 Which non-League club has a record 17 League team scalps in the FA Cup?

20 Which famous cricketer played for Antigua in the World Cup qualifiers?

Golden Oldies

Club mascots are usually youngsters – mainly under 10 years of age. But Swindon Town's mascot on 28 February 1996 was Bernard Ryan from Penhill – aged 50.

❁

The oldest player to appear in League football is Neil McBain on 15 March 1947 for New Brighton against Hartlepool United in Division 3 North. He kept goal at the age of 52 years 4 months. He was the club manager and an ex-centre half.

❁

Cyril Pontin of the Welsh League club Ponyclun broke his leg at the age of 43. He claimed still to be registered with the club as a player in 1995 at the age of 68.

❁

The oldest debutant in the League was A. Cunningham of Newcastle United. He played against Leicester on 2 February 1929 at the age of 38 years and two days.

David Seaman carries off Arsenal's mascot. His big smile was because he didn't have to carry Bernard Ryan. (Stewart Kendall/Sportsphoto)

On Top Of The World Cup

Path to the World Cup finals in 1970, El Salvador-style:

1 beat Honduras in a play-off in neutral Mexico City in a result that provoked the 'Four-Day War' between the countries.
2 lost to Haiti in second leg of next round after Haiti witch doctor sprinkled powder on the pitch.
3 beat Haiti in play-off in neutral Kingston, Jamaica, after coach Gregorio Bundio flattened witch doctor with a searing right hook to put him out of proceedings.
4 Bundio sacked after El Salvador qualified for finals.

❀

The most goals scored in a single World Cup finals competition is 13 by Frenchman Just Fontaine in 1958. The overall record is 14 goals by Gerd Muller of Germany in 1970 and 1974.

❀

A programme for the 1966 World Cup final would now sell for £30, which is 240 times its face value.

❀

The first goal in World Cup history was scored by Frenchman Lucien Laurent, who opened the scoring for his country against Mexico in the opening game of the first finals in 1930.

❀

Bryan Robson (England) is credited with the fastest goal in the finals, after 27 seconds of the match against France in 1982.

❀

*The photographer might think Roberto Baggio is flash,
but Madonna's just crazy for you.* (Colorsport)

Pop star Madonna was given the job of voting for the best-looking player in the 1994 World Cup finals. She voted for Roberto Baggio of Italy.

❀

The only player to score in successive World Cup finals is Vava of Brazil in 1958 and 1962. Pelé scored for Brazil in the 1958 and 1970 finals, and Paul Breitner, the German defender, scored in the 1974 and 1982 finals.

❀

Two people have both played in and then trained World Cup-winning sides. The Brazilian Mario Zagalo played in the 1958 and 1962 wins before coaching the 1970 side, and Franz Beckenbauer actually captained West Germany to success in 1974 before training his country's successful 1990 campaign.

❋

Henry Morris of Scotland gained his only cap against Northern Ireland on 11 October 1949. He scored a hat trick in an 8-2 win in Belfast and was never picked again. His first goal was the first scored by a British player in the World Cup.

❋

The first player to score in both the World Cup final and the Olympic Games final was Pedro Cea of Uruguay. He scored in the 1924 Olympic final in Paris and was on the mark six years later in the World Cup final.

❋

The Czech line-up for the 1934 World Cup final was made up entirely of players from the two Prague clubs, Sparta and Slavia.

❋

As is well known, Geoff Hurst is the only player to score a hat trick in a World Cup final, with three goals in 1966 against West Germany. What is less well known is that he repeated the feat in a 1985 charity game between the two teams at Elland Road as a fundraiser for the Bradford City fire disaster.

❋

Kazimierz Deyna, the Polish national captain, missed a penalty in the 1978 finals match with Argentina. He was celebrating his 100th cap.

❋

Antonio Cabrini, the Italian full back, was the first to miss a penalty in a World Cup final. He sent his shot wide against West Germany in the 1982 final, but Italy went on to win 3-1.

❋

Dino Zoff's left hand moves towards the mascot's bottom during the 1978 World Cup. (Colorsport)

In the 1982 finals Italy won the final, this despite not winning any of their group matches. They drew with Poland, Cameroon and Peru, but Paolo Rossi then found his scoring touch in the later stages.

⚽

Zaire keeper Muamba Kazadi was the first to be replaced for ineptitude. He was brought off after 22 minutes in the 1974 finals match with Yugoslavia and replaced by the reserve keeper Dimbi Tubilandu. Unfortunately, Dimbi proved to be an equal Dumbo by conceding a further six goals in a 9-0 defeat.

⚽

Daniel Xuereb (France) completed an A-Z of World Cup stars when he came on against West Germany in the 1986 finals. His appearance

Daniel Xuereb nearly falls over on hearing that he is the opening entry in the X-file in the World Cup's A–Z. (Popperfoto)

meant that every letter of the alphabet had been used in players' names in the World Cup finals.

❀

A Scottish referee on the 1958 World Cup panel was called Edward Charles Faultless.

❀

Pedro Gatica cycled from his home in Buenos Aires to support Argentina in the 1986 World Cup. When he arrived he couldn't afford the ticket to see the opening game. While he was negotiating his way into the ground, someone stole his bike.

❀

Before the days of more regimented numbering, Ossie Ardiles' number during the 1978 World Cup win was No 1, usually nowadays reserved for keepers. Argentina numbered their squad alphabetically.

England also numbered their squad for the 1982 World Cup finals in alphabetical order (apart from the goalkeepers), except for Kevin Keegan, who kept his favourite No 7 shirt.

A young Ossie Ardiles in action during the 1978 World Cup. (Colorsport)

I Wish I'd Said That

'But Dad, you don't know a thing about soccer.'
Philip Logan, 13-year-old son of the new US Major League Soccer commissioner

❀

'I take every day as it comes: I get up, I don't drink, I don't gamble, and I don't take drugs. Then I do the same tomorrow.'
Paul Merson, of Arsenal and England, on his battle to overcome various problems

❀

'I am thrilled to be the Scottish Writers' Footballer of the Year – now I'm not talking to you for six months.'
Paul Gascoigne announcing that he would continue his non-cooperation with Scottish journalists, despite the award

❀

'A team is like a nice clock, if just one piece is missing then the clock is still beautiful, but it doesn't work the same.'
Chelsea player-manager Ruud Gullit

❀

'If we'd bought all the players we've been linked with this summer, we'd need an extra dressing room.'
Joe Royle, Everton manager on the transfer speculation surrounding his club

❀

Klinsmann tries to pick up a Welsh swear word or two from Kit Symons during the European Championship qualifier between Germany and Wales.
(David Gadd/Sportsphoto)

'I was sent to find a weakness, and I found one – the half-time tea is awful.'
Shrewsbury coach Kevin Summerfield, sent to spy on FA Cup opponents Liverpool

David 'Ena Sharples' Beasant takes the term 'in goal' literally.
(Anton Want/Allsport)

'The fans nicknamed me Ena Sharples because my head was never out of the net.'
Raith Rovers keeper after conceding 10 goals in a Scottish Cup tie against Rangers

⚽

'Halfway through I hoped a hole would open up so I could jump in. But there'd be no room – half my team would have already been hiding there.'
Paul Sturrock, St Johnstone boss, after a 4-0 defeat at Stenhousemuir

⚽

'I can't do anything right. If I were to walk on water then they'd say that was because I couldn't swim.'
Berti Vogts, German trainer, before Euro 96 success

⚽

'If we had as many points as him we'd be in European football now.'
Manchester City manager Alan Ball on Garry Flitcroft's disciplinary record

❖

'Now I can enjoy my holidays.'
Eric Cantona on not being picked for Euro 96

❖

'I expect the next rule will ask us to play with one hand up our backside.'
Barcelona keeper Julen Lopetegui after hearing about FIFA's proposal to widen the goals

❖

'Why not put dwarfs in goal?'
French U21 trainer Raymond Domenech on the same FIFA ruling

❖

'It's the only job I have ever applied for in my life.'
George Best on his application to become Ireland manager after Jack Charlton's resignation

❖

George Best gets in some practice to see if he could ever make it as a waiter in a motorway service station. He decided not to apply.
(Mirror Syndication International)

'Downing 20 pints in a row.'
QPR striker Kevin Gallen when asked by the Ealing Gazette *what was his greatest achievement away from football*

❂

'We won't be able to call ourselves great until we have conquered Europe again.'
Sir Bobby Charlton on Manchester United's 1996 Double

❂

'I had a jersey with Thin on the back and Mrs Miklosko sewed a No 3 onto the jersey.'
Seventeen-year-old West Ham keeper Neil Finn, who made his debut in Ludek Miklosko's jersey (he wore No 1 with a 3 stitched on)

❂

'I'll only be a few minutes.'
BBC Radio 5 Live commentator Alan Green during the 1996 Derby v Leeds Cup tie when the PA at the Baseball Ground asked for an owner to move their car because the alarm was continually going off. Green was commentating to the nation at the time

❂

'We'll soon have to worry more about the court than goals and points.'
Franz Beckenbauer after the Bosman ruling

❂

'He's running the Magic Roundabout.'
A Bristol Rovers director on Birmingham boss Barry Fry's team selections

❂

'I scored at Anfield on the day Ian Rush broke the record, and they'll never take that away from me.'
Rochdale defender Peter Valentine on his own goal in the FA Cup at Anfield

❂

Stewards at Selhurst Park getting carried away by the atmosphere during a Wimbledon game. (Phil Cole/Allsport)

'This place is a morgue – the sooner we get to our new home in Dublin the better.'
Wimbledon manager Joe Kinnear on life at Selhurst Park as tenants of Crystal Palace

⚽

'It's a great honour, but I'd better pay my community charge first.'
Alan Knight, Portsmouth goalkeeper, after the Mayor suggested he be given the Freedom of the City

⚽

'The only thing he hasn't had this season is Mad Cow's Disease, but as he's a keeper there's still time.'
Reading manager Jimmy Quinn on Bulgarian captain Bobby Mihailov's injury problems

⚽

'Next time I go home I'll have a paper bag over my head.'
Blackburn's Geordie forward Graham Fenton after his two goals in the last four minutes scuppered Newcastle's championship hopes

⚽

'The referee was determined to see the game through – but if you don't have goalposts, a ball and a pitch, it's a bit of a struggle.'
Brighton manager Jimmy Case after rioters ended the match with York City after 16 minutes

⚽

'Southampton is a very well-run club from Monday to Friday. It's Saturdays we have problems with.'
Lawrie McMenemy, Southampton general manager

⚽

'You put flags on Everest and the North and South Pole – not on a pitch.'
Ali Sen, Fenerbahce chairman, after Graeme Souness, the Galatasaray manager, incited trouble by placing his club flag in Fenerbahce's centre circle to celebrate the cup final win

⚽

'I said to him – why didn't you just belt it.'
Barbara Southgate on her son's miss in the Euro 96 penalty shoot-out against Germany

⚽

'I wish I could say I don't know how it feels, but I'm afraid I do.'
Stuart Pearce to Gareth Southgate

⚽

'My wife said – take Oliver Bierhoff with you.'
Berti Vogts on his decision to include the Euro 96 winner as a late addition to his squad

'Will Mr Albert Clegg of Darwen please go home immediately; your whippet has just had pups.'
Blackburn Rovers tannoy

A messenger dog hurries across the pitch in 1969 to tell its owner that his wife has got his dinner on the table, and where is he?
(Mirror Syndication International)

What They Did Next

Ian St John said in 1969, having become a DJ for Radio Merseyside: 'I have no thoughts on taking up broadcasting when my soccer days are over. [Being a DJ] is only a hobby – football will always be my first choice.'

❄

West Brom goalkeeper Jim Cumbes set up a business, called 'Rent-a-Star', providing personalities for functions.

❄

Ron Clayton of Blackburn Rovers and England owned newsagents and gift card shops in Darwen, Blackburn and Nelson.

❄

Derek Dougan of Wolves became chairman of the Wolverhampton branch of the Mental Health Research charity.

❄

Alec Lindsay of Liverpool owned a pig farm in Bury.

❄

Matt Gillies, the Leicester City manager from 1959 to 1968, was also a magistrate.

❄

Spurs Double-winner Dave Mackay founded a company which made club ties.

❄

Alan Birchenall and Tony Currie kiss: 'Come up and see me, make me smile.'
(Mirror Syndication International)

A slaughterer at Aberdeen abattoir, Ron Yeats, went on to play for Dundee, Liverpool and Scotland.

⚽

Alan Birchenall, of Sheffield United, Chelsea, Crystal Palace and Leicester, used to sing with Joe Cocker.

Premier Trivia

Arsenal tube station was originally named Gillespie Road, but manager Herbert Chapman persuaded the tube authorities to rename it after the club in 1932. Two years before, he had failed in an attempt to rename the club Royal London.

⚽

Aston Villa's Peter Aldis is credited with the longest headed goal in a League game – from 35 yards against Sunderland on 1 September 1952. The previous record was also by a Villa player, Frank Barson, from 30 yards against Sheffield United on 26 December 1921.

⚽

Blackburn Rovers insist on good dress etiquette at their Ewood Park executive suites. One of the suites is rented by Wrangler Jeans.

Colin Hendry checks out Peter Schmeichel's shirt to see if it will pass the strict sartorial standards required at Ewood Park.
(Stewart Kendall/Sportsphoto)

The weathercock at Chelsea's Stamford Bridge is the likeness of George Hilsdon, who scored six goals in an FA Cup tie against Wolves in 1907-8.

❋

Coventry City were the first club to use CCTV. They attracted a crowd of 10,295 to watch the second division match against Cardiff City in October 1965 on closed-circuit TV at Highfield Road. The game was seen by 12,639 at Ninian Park, Cardiff.

❋

Derby County's ground was said to be cursed by gypsies after they were moved off the ground in 1895. Two years later they won a baseball match of national standing, hence the current name.

❋

Everton was the first club ever to record 10 or more away victories in a League season three years in succession, from 1984-5 to 1986-7.

❋

An official acoustics survey in 1995 revealed that Leeds United was the noisiest ground. Each League ground was visited three times and attendances also taken into account.

❋

Brian Deane's ears begin to hurt because of all the noise at Elland Road. (Paul McFegan/Sportsphoto)

When Leicester were founded in 1884, a collection to raise money for a ball netted just 9d.

Liverpool went a record 24 games without defeat in the League Cup after losing 1-0 to Bradford in August 1980, though they still won the trophy that season. Their run was ended by Burnley in the second leg of the semi-final in February 1983 – though, again, they won the cup that year, and also won it in 1984, too.

Manchester United's Steve Bruce is the only Englishman to have captained a side to the Double this century. Had he been fit for the 1996 FA Cup final, he would have matched his 1994 achievement.

When Middlesbrough were promoted to the first division in 1973-4 as champions of the second, their winning margin over second-placed Luton was 15 points – the biggest ever recorded under the old system of two points for a win.

Newcastle United once sold rosettes made from genuine mink.

The first rose in the world to be named after a football club was the 'Nottingham Forest'.

In their early days Sheffield Wednesday were known as The Blades – now the nickname of their rivals Sheffield United.

Southampton's deadly penalty taker Matt Le Tissier scored his most crucial penalty on 7 May 1994 against West Ham, as it helped secure the club's Premiership place. As if that wasn't enough pressure, the goal was his 100th in the League.

⚽

Sunderland went 60 years without an English manager until Alan Brown took the job in 1957.

⚽

Andy Turner, who scored his debut Premier League goal for Tottenham against Everton in September 1992, within a month of the league's opening, remains the youngest player ever to have scored in the Premiership at 17 years and 166 days.

⚽

Andy Turner, the youngest ever scorer in the Premier League. (Colorsport)

West Ham United's Upton Park is in *East* Ham.

⚽

Wimbledon are the only team to have won the Amateur Cup (in 1963) and the FA Cup (in 1988).

Packing Them In...or not

The highest official record attendance is 199,854 for the 1950 World Cup final between Brazil and Uruguay at the Maracana Stadium, Rio de Janeiro.

❖

The record attendance for a League match in England is 83,260 for Manchester United's home clash with Arsenal on 17 January 1948 at Maine Road, when Old Trafford was being rebuilt after war damage.

❖

The record attendance for a League game outside the top division is 70,305 at White Hart Lane on 25 February 1950 when Tottenham played Southampton.

❖

On 27 December 1949, a total of 1,272,185 spectators watched the 44 League matches – the highest-ever tally for a single day. That's an average of 28,913 per match.

❖

The lowest attendance for an FA Cup final is 20,740 for the 1901 replay between Tottenham Hotspur and Sheffield United at Burnden Park, Bolton.

❖

On 19 January 1957, no fewer than 18,069 people turned up to watch Wrexham Reserves against Wisford United – the attraction being that tickets were on sale for a forthcoming FA Cup tie with Manchester United.

❖

*It is important that police officers are constantly alert to spot
any sign of violence at a match, as demonstrated during this 1966
game between those low-key rivals Manchester United and Liverpool.*
(Mirror Syndication International)

When Chester City played at Macclesfield while their new Deva
Stadium was being constructed, police asked the home fans to stay in
their places while the away fans from Stoke, who considerably
outnumbered them, could leave first. It was not the only time that
particular tradition was broken.

❁

The lowest attendance for a League game is 13 between Stockport
County and Leicester City on 7 May 1921. The venue was switched to
Old Trafford.

❁

The lowest attendance for a British international match is 2,315 for
Wales v Northern Ireland at Wrexham on 27 May 1982.

❁

On 7 December 1990 the attendance for the fourth division game between Scarborough and Wrexham was just 625.

⚽

West Ham United were forced by UEFA to play their home Cup-Winners' Cup leg against the Spanish club Castilla (Real Madrid's nursery team) behind closed doors after crowd trouble in Spain where the Spaniards won 3-1. Each club could have a party of 70 (including players) and 16 ball boys were hired to collect the ball from the empty terraces. The media were also accredited. The official attendance was 262, and receipts were nothing. West Ham won the tie 5-1 with two extra-time goals, all six goals being greeted in stony silence and players being unsure whether they had scored.

⚽

Barcelona's Nou Camp stadium now has a capacity of 119,000 – all seated.

Two seagulls would have been a welcome addition to the 1990 match between Scarborough and Wrexham. (Empics)

Extra Time

1 Who won the 1996 Welsh Cup, from a population of 974?

2 Who scored in six successive England internationals in 1981-2?

3 Name the four clubs to have won all three European club competitions.

4 Which clubs from 1994-6 failed to gain entry to the League despite winning the Conference?

5 Stoke City play at the Victoria Ground, but which Scottish League team plays at Victoria Park?

6 Which is the only city to have witnessed top-division soccer in England continuously since the start in 1888?

7 Which club had a goals tally of 104 for and 100 against in 1957-8?

8 How many clubs have won back-to-back European Cup-Winners' Cups?

9 Who was the only substitute referee to appear during Euro 96?

10 And whom did he replace?

11 Who was the first reigning monarch to attend the FA Cup final – and when?

12 Which club did Maidstone United replace in the League?

A Brazilian fan prays that her nation will win the men's World Cup during the penalty shoot-out in the 1994 final - but who won the women's World Cup? (Action Images)

13 Which is the only club never to have been relegated from the top division?

14 Brazil are the current World Cup holders, but who are the current women's World Cup holders?

15 Which keeper commanded a world record transfer fee of £7.5 million?

16 Which club play their home games at Sixfields?

17 Which club has a world record 46 domestic championship titles?

18 In which city will the final of Euro 2000 be staged?

19 Name the two players tied on 31 goals who were the top scorers in the major European leagues in 1995-6.

20 Name the six players to have played for England since World War II with X in their surname.

Beat The Bar-room Bully – Answers
correct to 1 August 1996

1 Nancy Lorraine
2 They won the double in their respective countries
3 Burnden Park, Bolton Wanderers
4 Newport County
5 Malcolm Macdonald v Cyprus in 1975
6 29 occasions
7 Bradford Park Avenue
8 Arsenal in 1891
9 Bobby Moore
10 Johan Cruyff
11 Royal Engineers
12 Rochdale in 1962
13 They were drawn away in each round
14 Italy, France and Germany
15 Celta Vigo and Seville
16 Carsten Jancker of Rapid Vienna with 6 goals
17 Jurgen Klinsmann of Bayern Munich with 15 goals in the 1995-6 UEFA Cup
18 Spartak Moscow (then six players left!)
19 Tony Cascarino of Marseille
20 1961
21 True – lost twice each to AC Milan and Juventus
22 Alan Smith of Arsenal in 1989 and 1991
23 Reading
24 Bryan Robson with 90
25 Steve Death of Reading
26 Jim Leighton with 74 to the start of 1996-7
27 Mark Hateley of Rangers with 22 goals in 1993-4
28 Parkhead, Celtic FC
29 Bangor City, Wales
30 Eric Cantona – Auxerre, Montpellier, Marseille and Nimes

31 Alvin Martin for West Ham in their 8-1 win against Newcastle on 21 April 1986
32 Eoin Hand
33 Kaiserslautern
34 Notts County in 1995
35 Luxembourg
36 Gheorghe Hagi of Romania
37 1982 and 1984
38 Les Ferdinand
39 Cwmbran Town
40 Guy Goethals of Belgium – his father, Ray, trained Marseille to 1993 European Cup win

Mastermind – Answers

1 Gianfranco Zola
2 Rigobert Song of Cameroon, aged 17 in 1994
3 Sutton United
4 1985 – Trevor Francis and Graeme Souness for Sampdoria, Ray Wilkins and Mark Hateley for AC Milan
5 Crusaders of Northern Ireland
6 Malmo in 1979
7 Pelé – the real one won in 1973 in South America while Abdi Pelé was African Footballer of the Year in 1991, 1992 and 1993
8 Billy Wright
9 Liverpool in 1984 v Roma after a 1-1 draw
10 It was won on a golden goal
11 Hibernian
12 Jan Molby of Liverpool in the League Cup
13 1976
14 1959
15 Stade Reims
16 He was the first to train two World Cup-winning teams, in 1934 and 1938

17 Iain Dunn of Huddersfield v Lincoln in the 1994-5 Auto Windscreens Shield
18 Joe Mercer and Terry Venables
19 Yeovil Town
20 Viv Richards

Extra Time – Answers

1 Llansaintffraid
2 Paul Mariner
3 Juventus, Ajax, Barcelona, Bayern Munich
4 Kidderminster, Macclesfield, Stevenage
5 Ross County
6 Liverpool
7 Manchester City
8 None
9 Paul Durkin of England
10 Dermot Gallagher of England in the France v Bulgaria game
11 George V in 1914, when Burnley beat Liverpool at Crystal Palace
12 Darlington
13 Wimbledon
14 Norway beat Germany 2-0 in Stockholm on 18 June 1995
15 Gianluca Pagliuca, moving from Sampdoria to Inter Milan
16 Northampton Town
17 Glasgow Rangers
18 Amsterdam
19 Alan Shearer of Blackburn and Juan Pizzi of Tenerife
20 Albert Quixall, Lee Dixon, Graeme Le Saux, Kerry Dixon, Mike Duxberry and Graham Rix